I'm Not Broken

Casandra Matheson

BookLeaf
Publishing

Presentation by *BookLeaf Publishing*

Web: www.bookleafpub.com

E-mail: info@bookleafpub.com

ISBN: 978-93-95755-94-8

First edition 2022

DEDICATION

Isabella, Elijah, Christian, Isaac & Harrison...

You are the reason I wake, the reason I breathe and the reason I want to be better.

I love you all more than you will ever know.

Family

When you need to find yourself,
Don't drink the hatters tea;
It's full of lost thoughts forgetting,
And twisted memories.
When the caterpillar asks you,
Who you really are;
Take good care before you answer,
As a riddle, this one's hard.
Lay low around the red Queen!
She'll take all that ever mattered!
She'll leave you wishing you we're dead!
For goodness sake, do ignore the rabbit!
He'll only get you lost,
The price of his insanity;
It's far too high a cost,
It's not worth your mentality.
When it comes to Wonderland,
There's only one way to survive;
You've got to explore on your own,
Or you'll never leave alive.

Conditioned

I was raised by vicious wolves,
So excuse me if I'm savage;
Sometimes I know I may seem rough,
It just reflects my damage.
I'm trying to be civilized,
When I was never taught quite how...
When I finally get there,
Boy will you be proud!
Conditioned throughout my whole life,
To bite harder than I bark,
I'm the one to be scared of;
Not monsters in the dark.
If they hurt you,
Hurt them;
In the cruelest possible way,
That love was meant for family;
I learnt that's wrong, it's not okay!
They said women should be harder,
Than all the men that surround;
The truth is the men I grew up with,
Were nothing more than cowards.
The women think they're something great,
But truly it's a turn off ...
Who wants to come home to Suzie?

When she throws her weight harder than
Vercingetorix.
I'm learning to be softer,
Gentle to the touch;
Kinder with the words I use ,
(I know it doesn't seem like much).
To me it's a much higher feet,
Than any mountain known;
I wasn't raised,
I was conditioned;
Something I'm trying to outgrow.

Fighter

Good morning fighter,
You're stronger than you know;
Visibly wearing battle scars,
Braver for each on that you show.
Getting up each morning,
With the strength to face the day;
Despite all the pain inside,
Knowing it won't always be ok.
Brush the worry from your hair,
While dressing up with hope;
Once again it's crystal clear,
You have the strength to cope.
Lacing up your optimism,
While slipping on your smile;
All your dreams will come to fruition,
If you work for them a while.

Battles

Peace was not an option,
So a warrior she became;
Surviving every battle,
Until they feared her name.
Her soul was made of darkness ,
Or so every other thought;
She found it easier to hide her light,
If she simply shut it off.
Deep inside that flame does burn,
Although the darkness does conceal;
Even if peace was not an option,
It's still all she wants to feel.

Journey

Travelling down this long dark road
The days feel but like just minutes,
Pull over in the break-down lane;
To start what's not been finished.
Feelings get so hot and heavy,
I start to overheat.
For once my mind it does not race,
Head spinning from the meet;
And that look upon your face,
No Hazards call to me.
Emotions rush,
My heads a blur;
He wants me to promise ,
I won't get hurt-
So I make the side that feels,
Conceal it all not real..
Not quite sure what this moment is,
But I do know what's the deal.

Awakened

Realising your potential,
As we hit some brand new depths;
You make me feel appreciated,
With you there's no regrets.
We share in love and laughter,
Explosive energy;
You make me feel quite special,
Like a modern day lady.

With us there's no illusion,
We're aware of all the flaws;
It helps us to grow deeper,
Recognition to the core.
Let me cater to you now,
You deserve the best!
Let me show you how king's live,
Lay your head upon my chest.
Not quite sure how I met you,
I'm damn sure proud you're mine;
Wouldn't trade you for the world now,
I'd only buy your time.

If Only

If only you could borrow my eyes,
To see your inner beauty;
You'd appreciate every smile,
For what it is truly.
You'd feel the strength that radiates,
From the core so purely;
You'd hear the passion spoken softly,
If you'd listen closely.
If only you could borrow my ears,
You'd hear a heart so true;
One that's been hurt too many times,
One that's left you blue.
Yet everyday it beats alone,
Showing compassion and courage;
It's strong!
Almost as strong as you,
For love it's had to forage.
If only you could borrow my heart,
To see how you make me feel;
You'd never doubt my love again,
You'd know these feelings are so very real.
You'd feel the intensity of a love,
That burns so deep inside;
Then maybe you'd understand,
That just to know you is a blessing,
My exceptionally handsome man.

"love quotes"

I spent hours searching,
To show you how I feel;
Only problem is no one has ever loved,
The way I do ... It's surreal.
There's no words of reflection,
Encapturing how my souls alight;
It's like you've put a spell on me ,
Each and every night.
You are my siren song,
I know it may sound silly;
With every single note you play,
You're stringing me along.
So please do be careful,
Ive already lost love once;
Don't know if I could cope again,
But I'm taking the chance.

Jacked

You know you shouldn't climb it,
That beanstalk is not yours;
Yet it provides a sense of comfort,
And makes you feel secure.
Visible foundations shaky,
As the leaves fall on the floor;
Somehow you've found new height of lands,
You've never seen before.
The sights within your reach now,
So persistence never ends;
Once the horizon breaks into view,
It's clear there is no end.
Transcending past the chaos,
Escaping all fibers of your morals;
You reach for golden eggs not owned,
Even if it causes quarrels.
Running to escape...Your reality,
Before the beast hits home;
This life richer it might be,
Now you're feeling all alone.
Someone else's bridges burnt,
Now you question worth and value;
Of every lesson learnt,
Everything is all jacked up
You do not belong
Slide back down that beanstalk boy,
For here is not your home.

I'm Sorry!

It was pointed out tonight,
That I never do say sorry;
I won't admit when I am wrong,
Just "I miss you" or "I'm worried".
These words that passed were said in jest,
Like it was common knowledge;
By someone just in passing speech,
It took no effort ...nor no courage.
They know me well...to the core,
So the works effect;
They shook me more,
Than one would ever realise.

I am truly heartless,
Or I could see how that's what was thought;
So this right here's my sorry,
No stronger words were fought.
My ego gets the best of me,
My stubbornness does too;
But for every thing I say,
My actions mean well too.
I'm trying to be better,
I'm trying to be strong;
But still hold a gentle softness,
So that femininity is not gone.

Please forgive my arrogance,
It was never meant to fawn;
I am learning slowly,
But I'm doing it alone.

Still alive

Sometimes I wonder what I did,
To deserve to be torn down;
You took the time to plant me,
But where are you now ?
Where is the water or the sunlight ?
That I crave and need for life,
I'm just left alone now;
To wither and die...
Did you hear the screams ?
When I begged you all for help...
I think you chose to ignore them,
Too busy watering yourself.
Why didn't you replant me ?
My roots grew too big.
Did you want to confine me ?
Am I prettier like this ?
This is what you've envisioned,
But not all that I will be,
I've learnt to use these roots to walk;
I'm finally free.
I'll water my own garden bed,
As I bask in natural light;
One thing you didn't count on,
Is this flower has some fight.

Lessons

Each day brings romance,
But I'll never learn;
Exactly who is worth the chance,
And who is just to burn.
They just add to the mountain,
Of heartaches I've earned;
Some words once spoken,
Can not be returned.
Let this be the last,
Of the lessons I'll learn;
On my way to forever,
Watching all my bridges burn .

Felicia

I cut you off again today,
Damn it really hurt;
Once again I was blinded,
Didn't see what wouldn't work.
2 different paths met ways,
Now we sit drifting away;
If only feelings would reciprocate,
It would all just be ok.
They tell me that not everyone,
Bleeds with the same heart;
Now finally I can see,
That is why we were ripped apart.
Through good intentions it did start,
You led me down the garden path
Straight into the dark.
Pure words
Intent stares
Just empty promises
You didn't care.

Moonshine

I wish the moon could illuminate,
All the pain in my chest
You'd see the vast expanse of hurt;
Covering the nest.
Confusion and wonder,
Creep through my mind
Rhetorical questions;
I try to unwind.
Always in circles,
Path never clear
Do I stay;
Or do I go;
From all the love held dear.
I wish the moon could illuminate,
All the pain that's in my chest
Wash it all away tonight;
Replaced with peace and rest.

Caged

She caged her heart in barbwire,
It fit her like a glove;
Then covered her body in armour,
So not to be damaged by love.
She laced up metal boots,
As the eggshells she walks on;
Surely break,
While inwardly the voices,
Ask how much more she can take.
She knows she's a fighter,
One of the best they've ever seen;
Yet slowly she deteriorated,
Her eyes still held that gleam.
With her heart on her sleeve,
All that she wants;
Is one true love...someone to call home,
Yet every investment made
Leaves her alone.
How can she love,
With a body full of pain,
Everyone she's ever loved;
Pray on scars that do remain.
Never seeing her true beauty,
From her depths they do abstain;
They wonder why she seems so mean,
She whispers "never again"...

I'm ok ?!

The truth is ...
If I had a blade
Id cut the pain away
Scrambling in the endless darkness.
Somehow I've lost my way...
Identify fades as the selfless acts rise
Somewhere in the faceless clouds
My breathlessness does hide.
Mentally I won't stammer
Too burdened by my pride,
The war paint goes on daily
Slowly it does glide
As I make up my real eyes.

The voices of turmoil consume me now daily
As I make up the smile...red lips
I continue slowly I move on....fading
Mentally recluse as I'm ok leaves my lips.
The past eats my soul
As my love now does decay
The hoops clip my ears
As I make plans for the day.
I gather wounds
I thread the needle

All is fixed with a suture
Dressed now ready for the coffin
This seems to be my future
Consumed by the darkness
It's all I see now
My presence is bleakness
Stumbled once now infinately I sproal
Now forever they see my weakness.

Struggles

I wake up and the phone's off,
Foxtel now downgraded;
No milk left in the fridge today,
Man I feel like such a failure.
Shoulders weighed down,
By the burden of remorse;
4 kids under 5 I'm raising,
Do you really realise the cost ?
Getting by on bare essentials,
Yet they all think that I'm shining;
Shuffled one more disconnection,
Hell I'm barely surviving.
See the figures are way the negative,
When you can't rely on dad;
It's worth it for a peace of mind,
That I may not have had.

Daddy

What if you moved your stuff back home,
And it actually fucking worked;
What if loving each other deeply,
Didn't have to hurt.
What if everything we've dreamed together,
Actually came true;
What if we could be a family,
Not broken...missing you.
What if at the end of each night,
I could hold you in my arms;
What if you had a problem,
For once I could help not harm.
What if the picket fence was white,
And the Sunday's were all ours;
What if I could say you were mine again,
Damn I'd be so proud.
What if you could watch your son grow,
Each and every day;
He could wake up to his daddy,
Life would never be the same.

Hell

Hell is real
It is encompassed in my heart
Deep Beneath the surface
The demons proudly hark
Devour the endless trauma
Seeking solice In the dark
My soul they slowly conquer
Silent whispers through my art
The light it does fade daily
As my soul is ripped apart
True self but a memory
As words of hope fail to spark
Family but a word now
Severed with the frost
Love is a word I won't allow
The devil says it's lost.

Villains

In an instant it all clicks,
Perspective is now clear;
No longer hiding,
Or suppressing pent up fear.
Lines drawn for the battle,
Overstepping the enemies mark;
All white flags drawn now blood stained,
With the bleeding of our hearts.
Justice in clear view now,
As it all falls in my hands;
The cross I bare, my privilege,
The weight to bare no man's.
Where the law repeatedly failed,
I'll no longer succumb;
To an empire full of males,
This Queen is number one.
Muster all inner strength passed,
To lead my first front line;
This war will be my first and last,
Even if the path is not Devine.
The means justifies the cause,
All to see the villain's lost;
Everything I once stood for,
Fate now mine to chose.

Smile

She flips through old pictures,
At the smile she once wore;
The smile that everyone complimented,
Wasn't hers anymore.
She recognised it faintly,
As the feelings she once had;
She hadn't seen it lately,
But God she wished that she had.

See the day she left Sydney,
Along with everyone she loved;
She did it for her babies,
Her heart was not thought of.
Now she sits here lonely,
Not a smirk in sight;
It somehow all seems worth it,
To have them by her side.
How I miss that smile,
And the ones who put it there;
I hope one day she finds that smile,
As it was made to share.